ARCH BOOKS
TREASURY

Vintage Collection
1964–1965

THE ORIGINAL 12 ARCH BOOKS

ARCH BOOKS

TREASURY

Vintage Collection
1964–1965

ARCH
BOOKS ®

CONCORDIA PUBLISHING HOUSE • SAINT LOUIS

Arch® Books

Published 2015 by Concordia Publishing House

3558 S. Jefferson Ave., St. Louis, MO 63118-3968

1-800-325-3040 · **www.cph.org**

Manufactured in Shenzhen, China/055760/300560

1 2 3 4 5 6 7 8 9 10   25 24 23 22 21 20 19 18 17 16 15

TABLE OF CONTENTS

ARCH BOOKS
TREASURY
Vintage Collection
1964–1965

Dear Parents,

Let the children come to Me, and do not hinder them,
for to such belongs the kingdom of God.

Luke 18:16

Parents and educators are given the wonderful responsibility of teaching children about God and His will for them. One of the ways we do this is by teaching them God's Word—the Bible. From its beginning in the mid-1960s to today, Arch Books have existed for the sole purpose of teaching the Bible to children. More than 400 different Arch Books have been published so far. And through them, millions of children have learned about biblical people and events, about faith and forgiveness, and about the Gospel of Jesus Christ.

Now, as this beloved series enters its sixth decade, Concordia Publishing House is re-releasing the first twelve Arch Books to commemorate its legacy and to celebrate its influence on Bible literacy. This collection is a reproduction of the original words and pictures that launched the series.

To God be the glory!

The editor

QUALITY RELIGIOUS BOOKS FOR CHILDREN

ARCH BOOKS

THE GOOD SAMARITAN

THE STORY OF THE GOOD NEIGHBOR

THE
GOOD
SAMARITAN

THE
GOOD
SAMARITAN

Luke 10:25-37 FOR CHILDREN

Written by Janice Kramer

Illustrated by Sally Mathews

Concordia Publishing House
St. Louis, Missouri

Over in the Holy Land,
so many years ago,
a merchant from Jerusalem
went down to Jericho.
He started out one lovely morn
as dawn began to break;
his little donkey carried
all the things he had to take.

The trip was rather pleasant
as they went down their way;
the merchant thought of all the things
that he would do that day.
He had some goods to trade and sell
and many things to buy;
he hoped to get to Jericho
before the night drew nigh.

But little did the merchant know
that farther down the road
a band of robbers eyed with greed
the little donkey's load.
Alert, with evil hearts, they watched
and waited till at last
the unsuspecting merchant and his beast
were walking past.

The leader of the bandits
gave a terrifying shout,
and with this sign the thugs emerged
and suddenly jumped out.

With great big clubs they beat the man;
they beat him till he bled,
then took his donkey, stole his goods,
and left him almost dead.

A silence settled over all,
the merchant was alone;
he lay there suffering by the road,
and no one heard him moan.
Too weak and dazed to help himself,
all he could do was wait;
would no one come along to help
before it was too late?

But down the road there came a man,
and he was drawing near;
at last the bleeding merchant thought
that help was really here!

It was a priest in purple robes,
hands folded as in prayer;
a priest would help the wounded man,
a priest would surely care!

His shuffling footsteps on the road
produced the only sound
while silent was the wounded man
so helpless on the ground.
The priest was busy praying,
his eyes were both shut tight.
But one eye chanced to open
and saw the sorry sight.

"Oh, what a shame!" the priest observed;
"I cannot stop today,
or I'll be late for service.
I must be on my way!
I'm sure that someone will come soon,
so I'll just let him lie."

And carefully
and quietly
he tiptoed right on by.

The merchant was alone again;
was this to be the end?
But then another man came down
the road and round the bend.
He was a Levite,* who helped the priests,
he sure would understand
that here and now he ought to stop
and lend a helping hand.

*A temple assistant

The Levite halted in his tracks,
his eyes grew very wide.
His heart was warm with pity
and felt a pain inside.
He stood there undecided;
he knew he ought to stay,
but what he really wanted was
to turn and run away.

"This truly is a horrid sight,"
the troubled Levite said.
"I really do believe he ought
to be at home in bed.
But I'm no doctor, mercy me,
I might do something wrong!
Besides,

I feel quite sick myself —
I'd better run along."

The day was drawing to an end,
and night was coming on;
the merchant now would surely die,
for every hope was gone.
But as the shadows of the night
displaced the light of day,
another man came down the road
by which the merchant lay.

This man was from Samaria,
his people long had been
despised and hated by the merchant
and all his countrymen.
The chance that this Samaritan
would help was very slim;
he surely wouldn't want to help
a man who hated him!

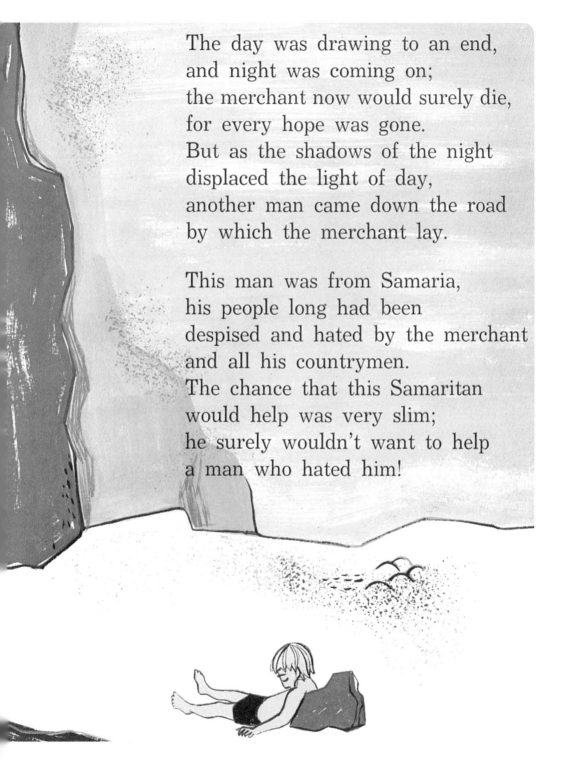

But as he came around the bend,
he stopped with great surprise;
for when he saw the merchant there,
he hardly could believe his eyes.
"How can it be? This wounded man
is out here all alone;
I would have come here sooner, friend,
if I had only known!"

And then the kind Samaritan
got down upon his knee;
he tried the very best he could
to help his enemy.

He gently bound each bloody wound
and tried to ease the pain;
oh, surely, it would be too bad
if he had helped in vain!

But when he'd given all the help
that he knew how to give,
he saw that now, without a doubt,
the wounded man would live!
He gently placed the merchant on
his donkey's back, and then
the two men and the donkey small
went down the road again.

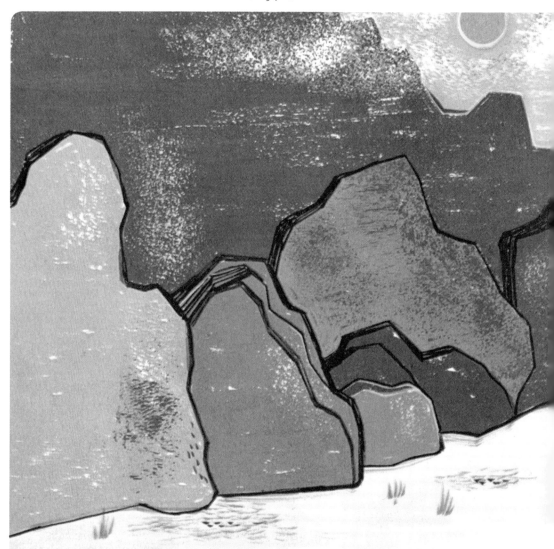

They had to travel very slow.
It was a lonely night.
At last this kind Samaritan
beheld a welcome sight.

He saw a warm and cozy inn
beside the road ahead;
he took the merchant to the inn
and put him right to bed.

Before the good Samaritan
went on along his way,
he paid the keeper of the inn
to let the merchant stay.
"Be sure to take good care of him," he
    said,
"for I intend
to pay in full, when I return,
for everything you spend."

"Now," asked our Lord,
"*Who* helped his fellowman
in every way he could?
Who was the one who acted here
the way a *neighbor* should?"
The priest, you'll say, was not the one—
he hurried right on by;
nor did the Levite help the man—
he seemed afraid to try.

The good Samaritan—he was
the only one to stay;
and though the merchant hated him,
he helped him anyway.
How wonderful if you and I
and all God's children would
show such a love to all we meet
as Jesus said we should!

Dear Parents:

We are to love our neighbor, the Great Commandment tells us. What does this mean? Does this include people who are not one of us, those of another race and religion, those who look down on us or we on them?

Because people were confused about this, Jesus told our parable. The hero of the story is a member of a people despised and hated by Jesus' nation because the Samaritans' race and religion were not pure.

Can you help your child understand the lesson taught in this parable? Can you help him carry out the sometimes difficult task of being a true neighbor, as the Samaritan was, even to those who may not seem our brothers, our "neighbors"? You may want to read to your child, or help him read it himself, the story of the Good Samaritan in your Bible (Luke 10:30-37).

THE EDITOR

QUALITY RELIGIOUS BOOKS FOR CHILDREN

ARCH BOOKS

THE BOY WHO RAN AWAY

THE PARABLE OF THE PRODIGAL SON

THE BOY WHO RAN AWAY

LUKE 15:11–32 FOR CHILDREN

Written by Irene Elmer
Illustrated by Sally Mathews

Concordia Publishing House
St. Louis, Missouri

There was a family once,
with two sons.
The older son
did what needed doing.

The younger son
did
what he liked.

He said,

"I had rather not be part of the family."

But

you need money

to do what you like.

The younger son had a bright idea.
He asked his father
for

half
of the family's money.

That was his share.

Then he went away

to do what he liked
with it.

He did not spend it

wisely.

Pretty soon

it
was
all
gone.

He wondered
why nobody liked him any more.

There had been no rain all year.
The ground dried up.
Plants died.

There was little to eat.
People begged him for money,
but he had no money left
to give.

He had to beg, too.

And nobody would give him
a piece of bread,
even.

Finally, he got a job
feeding pigs.

It was the only job
there was.

It was not an agreeable job.

And he was so hungry
he went after the pig food
and ate it.

He said to himself,
"I wanted to do what I liked,
        but now look at me.
Is this what I like?"
he said.
"No."

He said, "I had better go home to my father.
I will say, "Father, you can't let me be
an important part of the family now,
like a son,
but you might let me be
a small part,
say a servant." "

He went home.

But his father . . .

... saw him as soon as he got near the house.
And he ran out and kissed him,
because he was so glad
to get him back.

The son was ashamed to be treated
like an important part of the family.
He started to say
he could only be a small part now,
say a servant.

His father didn't listen.
He was too happy.

He sent for the best clothes
to dress him.

And he gave a big party,
with dancing and lots to eat.
He said, "My younger son
is part of the family again."

But the older son said,
"I'm part of the family, too.
And I always have been,
and you never gave a party for me."

"Why couldn't he?" their father said.
"I love him after all the things he's done."

"Of course. But you're his father."

"And, what do we call God?"

"Our Father," said the older son. "Oh . . . !"

"You see?", their father said.

"But I still don't see why you want to have a party!"

"Because our family is back together.
Isn't it a day to celebrate?
Come, let's welcome him!"

Dear Parents:

The parable of the boy who ran away from home (the Prodigal Son) was told by Jesus to explain and defend His receiving scoundrels and bad women among His friends and so into the kingdom of God (Luke 15:11-32; Matt. 11:19; 21:31). He took them in without a grudge or reproach and feasted with them.

Our story shows that since God is our loving Father, He acts the way Jesus did.

The parable is also an appeal to the member of God's family who had never run away but had faithfully served and obeyed his father all these years to receive his returning brother and take him in with joy.

Can you help your child think of God as just this kind of loving Father? And help him not to shut out the other child who may not have been as good as he and who wants "to make good"?

You may want to read to your child the full version of the parable in the New Testament, Luke 15:11-32.

THE EDITOR

QUALITY RELIGIOUS BOOKS FOR CHILDREN

THE GREAT SURPRISE

ARCH
BOOKS

The
Story of
Zacchaeus

THE GREAT SURPRISE

Luke 19:2-10 for children

Written by Mary Warren

Illustrated by Betty Wind

Concordia Publishing House
St. Louis, Missouri

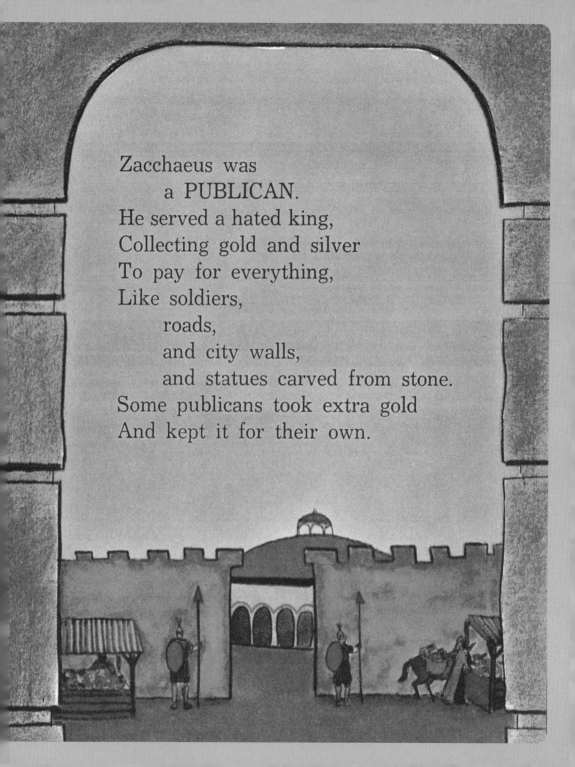

Zacchaeus was
    a PUBLICAN.
He served a hated king,
Collecting gold and silver
To pay for everything,
Like soldiers,
    roads,
    and city walls,
    and statues carved from stone.
Some publicans took extra gold
And kept it for their own.

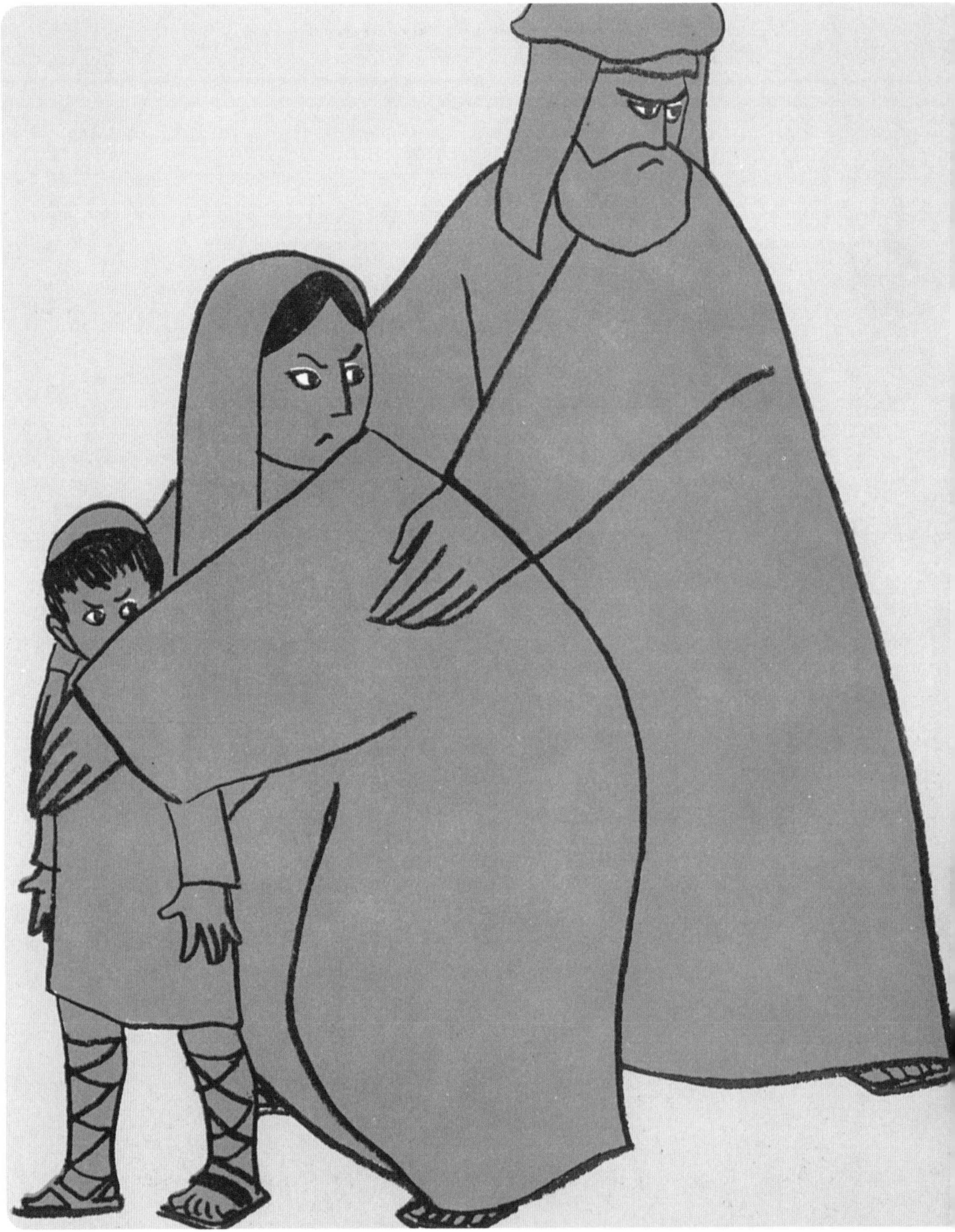

Most people hated publicans.
They said:
 "They're mean!"
 "They cheat!"
And so good people turned away
Whenever they would meet
The publicans around the town
Or walking down the street.

When Jesus met a publican,
He smiled and greeted him.
He didn't care
    what others thought
Or if they acted grim.
He loved all kinds of people:
He was friendly with the mean,
    the selfish,
        and the sickly,
            and those who
                were not clean.

He knew so many couldn't choose
The sort of life they had,
And many others didn't know
That they were being bad;
And even if they knew inside,
It made his heart feel sad.

Zaccheus once was going home
When there, along the way,
He saw a crowd and, curious,
He thought he'd rather stay.

"You say this man is Jesus?
May *I* get near to see?
I want to know what He is like...
But— OW! You're trampling me!

"Please tell me what this huddle
And this muddle is about!"
He begged,
    and teased,
    and pushed,
    and squeezed,
And then began to shout:

"I'm chief collector
for the King!
How *dare* you
leave me out!"

Zacchaeus ran and climbed a tree.
He wished he weren't so small;
But Jesus saw him there and stopped.
Zacchaeus heard Him call:
"Come down, Zacchaeus, right away,
And take Me home with you!"

The people stared with angry looks
And some began to stew.
They muttered, "What a place to pick–
The home of such a fake!

Don't tell us Jesus doesn't know—
He *does*, for goodness sake!
It is a mystery to us...
The friends He likes to make!"

Zacchaeus climbed down happy
With a sparkle in his eyes.
He shivered from excitement.
He felt a bigger size!
It made him feel so popular!
A messenger soon ran
      ahead to tell the news of this
To all Zacchaeus' clan.

A feast they started to prepare:
The servants roasted meat.
When Jesus got there later on,

One washed His dusty feet;
Another brought a lovely robe.
Then it was time to eat.

It took a while to eat such food!
They sat and talked, and when

Zaccheus saw how Jesus' love
Could change the hearts of men,

He said to Jesus:
    "I don't think
Of anyone but me!
The extra money that I take,
It's very plain to see,
Makes others poor,
    and here I sit
As wealthy as a king!
Before another day goes by,
I'll do an honest thing.

"My clothes and food
and all I own
I shall divide in two.
I'll take half to
the poorer folk
And . . . *I* know what I'll do!
What I owe to any man
I'll multiply by four.
I'll start to pay
my debts today,
And I will cheat no more!"

His children shouted out:
    "Hurrah!"
    "I'll share some toys of mine!"

His wife and servants also cheered:
"We think this sounds just fine!"

When Jesus rose to leave, He said:
"I've had a splendid stay!
Zacchaeus, it does give Me joy
To know you feel this way,
And you will find that this has been
A very special day!"

Dear Parents:

The religious people around Jesus were puzzled and angered by Jesus' associating with men of the worst past and His opening for them the doors of the kingdom of God. They said Jesus' behavior made light of God's holiness and His commandments.

Jesus reminded them of the care with which a person would look for one lost piece of silver or a single lamb and of the great joy when the lost is found again. It is because God feels this way about stray members of His human family that He sent Jesus to look for those who were lost.

Our story is a telling illustration of how Jesus related to those whom others had given up. He did not hesitate to reach out to them. He did not care what anyone would think of it, whether a person had deserved it or knew how to take it. He made no conditions to Zacchaeus before He would stay with him. The Gospel does not even record Jesus' scolding Zacchaeus for his past. It was Jesus' visit that made Zacchaeus say what no one except Jesus would have expected: "I will give half of my goods to the poor . . ." Jesus rejoices: "Today salvation has come to this family."

Can you help your child to understand that God's love is so great that He accepts us even when our actions are not acceptable? That God opens up His arms to us without making us meet any conditions first? That God loves this way both us and anyone else who has been bad, so that we, too, may not shut out such a person?

THE EDITOR

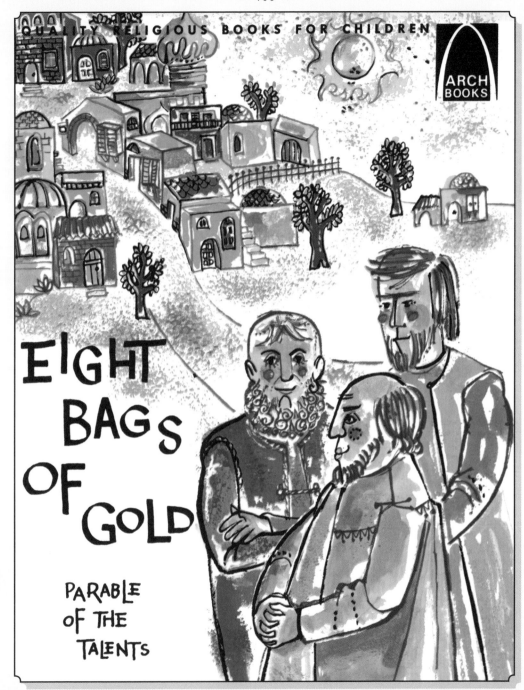

QUALITY RELIGIOUS BOOKS FOR CHILDREN

ARCH BOOKS

EIGHT BAGS OF GOLD

PARABLE OF THE TALENTS

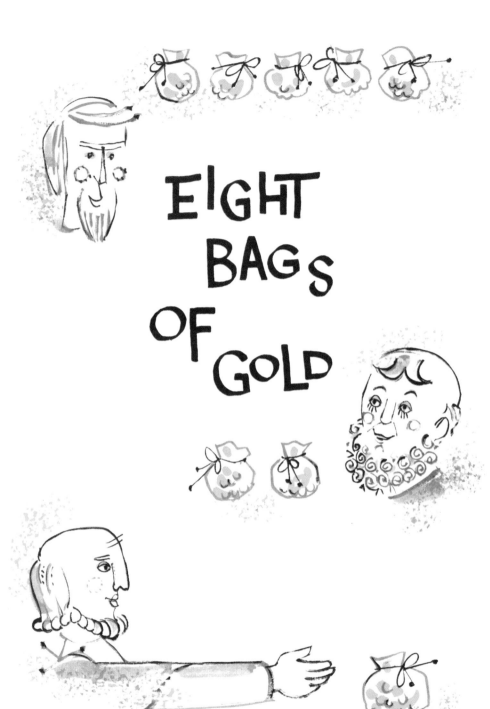

EIGHT
BAGS
OF
GOLD

EIGHT BAGS OF GOLD

Written by Janice Kramer
Illustrated by Sally Mathews

MATTHEW 25:14-30 FOR CHILDREN

Concordia Publishing House   St. Louis, Missouri

master's house

Once there was a master
well known throughout the land.
He had a hundred servants
who were under his command.

His house had many, many rooms,
and no one could deny
that he was rich, and there was not
a thing he couldn't buy.

One day the wealthy master
had important news to tell,
and so he called three servants
with a shiny silver bell.
The servants started running
when they heard the master's call;
until they reached the master's room,
they didn't stop at all.

They found the master waiting,
and they noticed at his side
a massive heap of precious gold
tied up in bags of hide.
"Ahem!" (The master cleared his throat.)
"I've called you here today
to tell you that I am about
to travel far away.

"The trip will be a long one,
so I think it's plain to see
that someone surely has to keep
these bags of gold for me.
I've thought and thought for many days,
and now I've hit upon
the answer to my problem —
YOU will keep them while I'm gone!"

He pointed to the servant
who was standing first in line:
"Come here," he said,
"and you shall have
your share of what is mine.
I give you these five bags of gold
to do with as you choose.
So then, till I return again,
these coins are yours to use."

Then to the second man he gave
two bags of gold and said:
"To make good use of all this wealth
you'll have to use your head."

The servant who was last in line
approached the master's chair.
"There's one bag left," the master said,
"and that will be your share.

"Now go, but don't forget,
when I return, I'll want to see
what faithful stewards you have been
in using it for me."
The servants made a bow so low
their foreheads touched the floor,
and then they gathered up their gold
and headed for the door.

The man who had five bags of gold
went out with troubled thought,
and in his mind he counted up
the things that could be bought!
"It's such a task — I must not fail!"
the puzzled servant sighed,
but then a plan popped into mind.

"That's what I'll do!" he cried.

"I'll buy a store, a great big store —
I'll sell so many things!

Like pots and pans
and shoes and coats

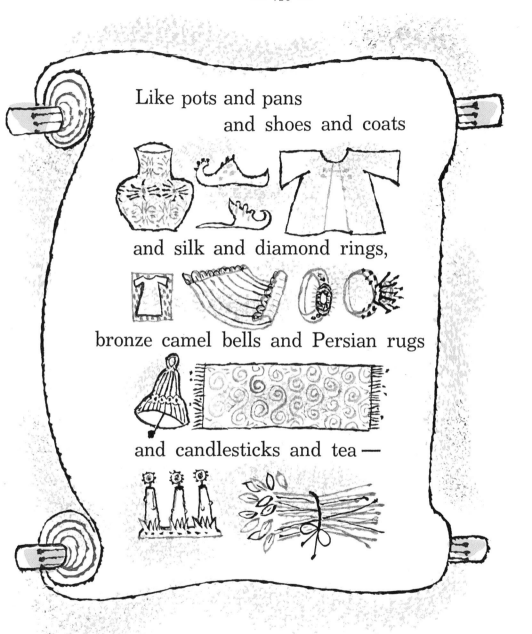

and silk and diamond rings,

bronze camel bells and Persian rugs

and candlesticks and tea —

the biggest store in all the land,
that's what my store will be!"

He bought a store, and people came
from places all around;
they came from almost every place
where people could be found

to buy the things they needed
in this store that was so grand,
for it was soon the superstore,
the biggest in the land!

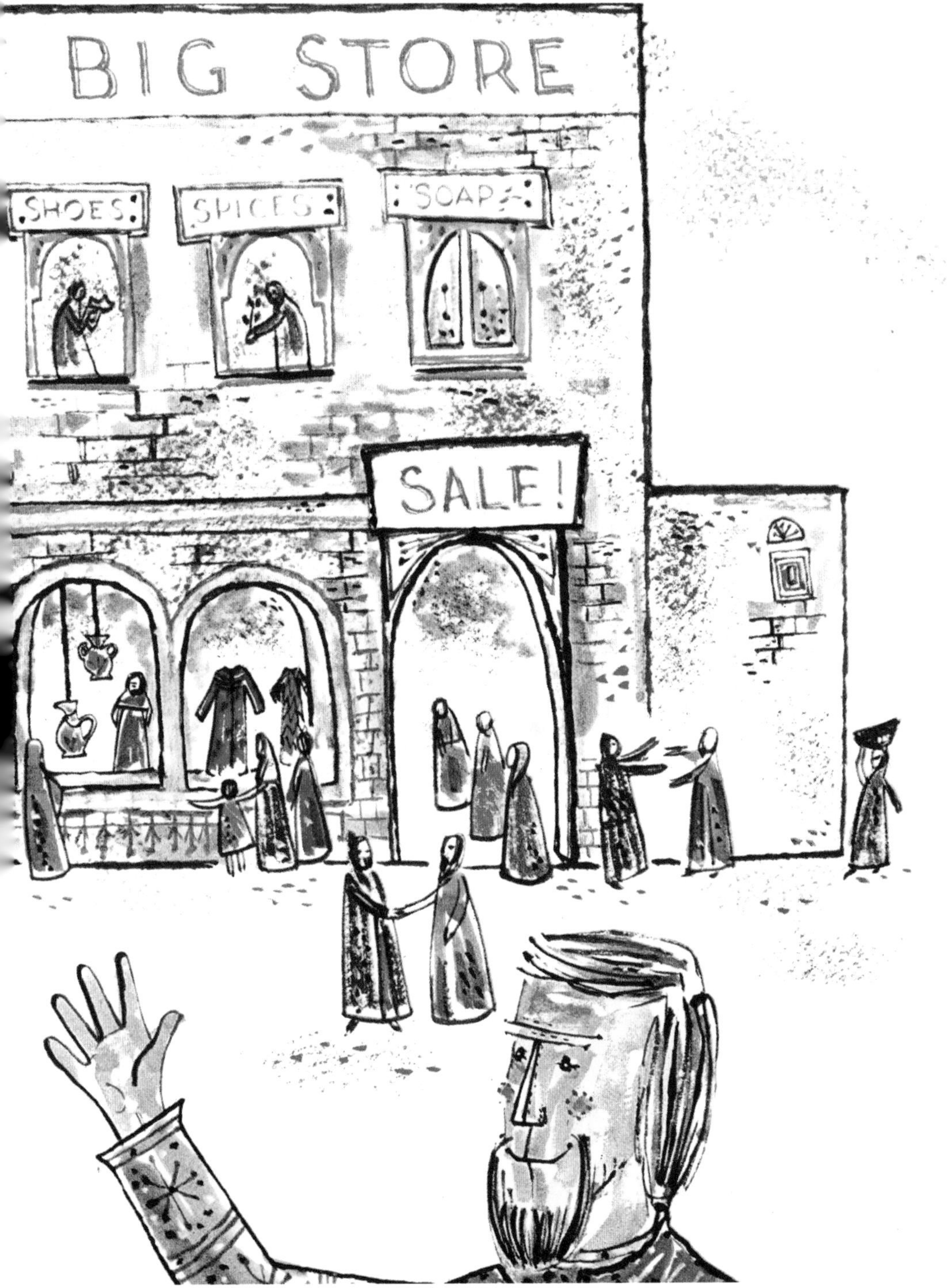
BIG STORE
SHOES
SPICES
SOAP
SALE!

And on the other side of town,
where shoreline meets the sea,
the man who had two bags of gold
was happy as could be.
For many years this servant
had possessed a secret wish:
to be the owner of a shop
for thriving trade in fish.

And so a marketplace for fish
was just the thing he bought,
and fishermen came in to sell him
all the fish they caught.

FISH FOR SALE

Then he in turn sold all the fish
to people of the land,
and so his business day by day
went on as he had planned.

For though he never had a crowd
around his little shed,
his marketplace did pretty well,
it truly must be said.
He didn't make a fortune
in his work of selling fish,
but still his marketplace fulfilled
his every dream and wish.

Now ever since his master
had departed on his way,
the man who had one bag of gold
had worried night and day.

"Oh, dear," he cried, "the gold I have
is such a small amount!
The coins my master gave to me
take little time to count.

"If I should use it — I might lose it! —
that would be the end!
I think he trusted it to me
to hide but not to spend."

And so that night he took his gold
and, quiet as a mouse,
he headed through the darkness
to an old, abandoned house.

Beneath the cellar floor he hid
the bag of gold secure.
"No one will ever find it here;
of that I can be sure."
Then up the stairs and through the door
into the night he ran.
"That spooky house," he panted,
"would sure scare the bravest men!"

The master then returned to town
and called his servants three:
"What have you done while I was gone?
I cannot wait to see."

The man who had received five bags
with pride stepped up and said,
"I bought a store, and now I have
ten bags of gold instead."

Then said the man who owned the shop
down by the ocean shore,
"You gave two bags of gold to me,
and I have gained two more."

"How wonderful!" the master said,
"and I am pleased to tell
you both that you shall have more gold
because you did so well!"

The man who had one bag of gold
came forward then and told
how he, to keep his treasure safe,
had hidden all his gold.
"Beneath the ground I buried it
and left it till today,
and here it is, the same amount
as when you went away."

"You foolish servant!" cried his lord,
as angry as could be.
"That you weren't brave with what you had
does not go well with me!

I wanted you to use it,
not hide it in a hole.
To do the best with what you had,
that should have been your goal."

The sad but wiser servant knew
he'd made a great mistake:
The master's gold was given
with a task to undertake.

His job was not to hide the gift
but use as best he could;
and if he failed, the master would
no doubt have understood.

Dear Parents:

This is a parable of Jesus.

It tells us that God expects us to make use of what He has given us in life.

He has given each of us different gifts. Some people can do things well with their hands, some with their heads, some with their voices; some can see things others don't.

Each of us is responsible to God for using the gifts he has from Him and for using them well.

In this parable Jesus gives encouragement to those who have gifts which seem small or few in comparison with the gifts others have. The master evidently had expected something even from the man with the one bag of gold. He was deeply disappointed that the servant had not even tried.

Can you help your child understand the meaning of the story? Will you help him also see and want to use the gifts God has given him and have confidence with regard to what he can do with them?

THE EDITOR

the RICH FOOL

A PARABLE OF A MAN AND HIS TREASURES

ARCH BOOKS

THe RICH FOOL

The RICH FOOL

Written by Janice Kramer
Illustrated by Sally Mathews

LUKE 12:16-21 FOR CHILDREN

Concordia Publishing House
St. Louis, Missouri

A long time ago, in a land far away,
there lived a rich man who did nothing all day
but to think and to worry, to hope and to plan
some way of becoming a wealthier man.

From his house to his fields
each day he would walk
to look at his crops —
every leaf, every stalk.
Then he'd climb to the top
of his great storage bin
where he kept all his grain,
and he'd sit there and grin.

He watched as his slaves labored hard in the sun
to put grain in the bin, loading ton after ton.

As he carefully counted the loads as they came,
he would think of his riches,
his wealth, and his fame.

A few hungry birds in the skies overhead
saw the big bin of grain, and downward they sped.
Oh, how happy they were!
For at last they could eat.
They landed and started to dine on the wheat.

But when the rich man saw them eating his grain,
he screamed and he kicked and waved his big cane.
"You can't have what's mine!
Get away from my bin,
or I'll hit you so hard your heads all will spin!"

He swung with such force
that he fell from his ladder
  right into the bin — and this made him madder!
With all of his wriggling and squirming around,
some of the grain poured out to the ground.

"My grain, oh, my grain!"
he snorted and sputtered.
"It can't be wasted — it can't," he muttered.
And then in a frenzy he looked all about
to see just how much of his grain had spilled out.

A poor man had started to pick up the wheat,
for his wife and six children had nothing to eat.

"Stop it, you thief,"
cried the rich man, alarmed,
and the poor man went running
for fear he'd be harmed.

The rich man saw all of the wheat that was spilt —
a new place for grain would have to be built.

"I'll tear down the old one," he said gleefully,
"and make bigger bins — how grand they will be!"

His slaves worked hard, his slaves worked long
to make the new bins big and strong.
The master from his platform high
surveyed their work with watchful eye.

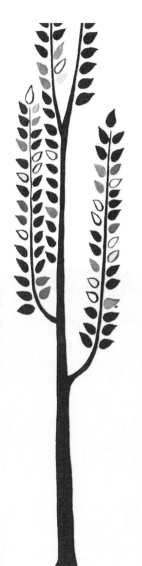

And when the job was finally done,
the night had come, gone was the sun.
He hurried home all full of pride —
as full as the bins
with his grain inside.

He went to his room and looked in the mirror.
He talked to himself, and he saw a good hearer.

"I really am a remarkable guy!
My riches will last till the day I die.

"I'll wear fine clothes
that are made of gold thread,
with gems on my belt, on my hands, on my head.
I'll eat and I'll drink, I'll dance and be gay,
and plan bigger things the rest of the day."

With a yawn and a stretch he turned to his bed.
"I'll think of my future tomorrow," he said.
Then looking once more at each wonderful bin,
he drew up the covers and tucked himself in.

The lamps on the bins
shone down through the night
to warn the rich man if thieves came in sight.
His treasure of grain was part of his plan
to be each day a much richer man.

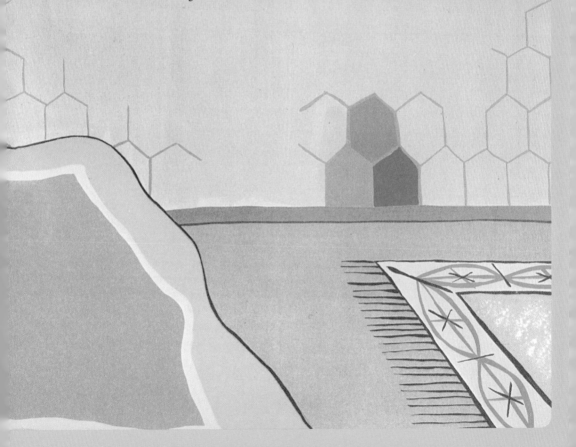

"Someday," he said, "I'll start anew
and live as God would like me to.

But first things first — myself I'll please
and live my life in wealth and ease."

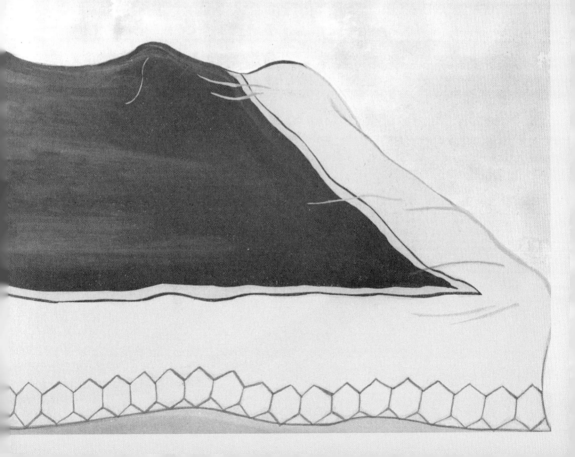

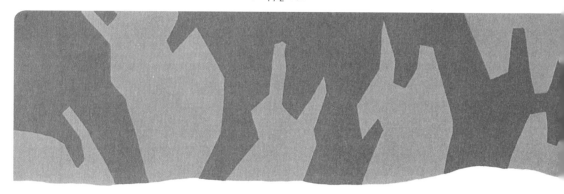

But that very night he died in his sleep,
with no one to mourn him and no one to weep.
This man had been selfish with all of his wheat;
he had offered no grain for the hungry to eat.

"How silly the rich, greedy man was!" you say.
Yes, he was silly, and right to this day,
because he was selfish and heartless and cruel,
he's not called the rich man —
he's called the rich fool.

Dear Parents:

The aim of our story isn't to create fear but to show how foolish it is to think the way this farmer did. It is important for us to understand and to help our children understand that Jesus isn't saying that we shall die if we are selfish but that it is senseless and foolish to think our belongings can insure us a happy life and future.

Our security lies in God. We are His children. He cares for us and provides what we need. Will you help your child to sense this in the way you teach him to look at life?

The Editor

QUALITY RELIGIOUS BOOKS FOR CHILDREN

ARCH BOOKS

LITTLE BENJAMIN AND THE FIRST CHRISTMAS

A BETHLEHEM BOY AND THE CHRIST CHILD

LITTLE BENJAMIN AND THE FIRST CHRISTMAS

LUKE 2:1 — 18 FOR CHILDREN

Written by Betty Forell
Illustrated by Betty Wind

Concordia Publishing House
St. Louis, Missouri

Benjamin watched the people coming into Bethlehem. What a lot of people there were! The king had ordered them to come to Bethlehem to be counted.

Some of them stayed in Benjamin's father's inn. Soon all the rooms were taken.

The inn was full of noise and excitement. "Here, boy, bring some hay for our donkeys!" they called out to Benjamin.

Finally Father locked the gate. No more room. Not even a corner. The family was tired and hungry. Supper smelled good. Father led them in their evening prayers. He read from the great prophet Isaiah:

"The people who walked in darkness have seen a great light. . . . For to us a Child is born. . . . , the Prince of Peace."

Father told the children what the words meant. "God has promised to send us a very special Prince to rule over all people and save us from wars and bad kings. In His kingdom all people will live together in love and peace."

"When will this Prince come?" Benjamin sighed. "This is such an old promise from God. Will it ever come true? Will I ever get to see the wonderful Prince?"

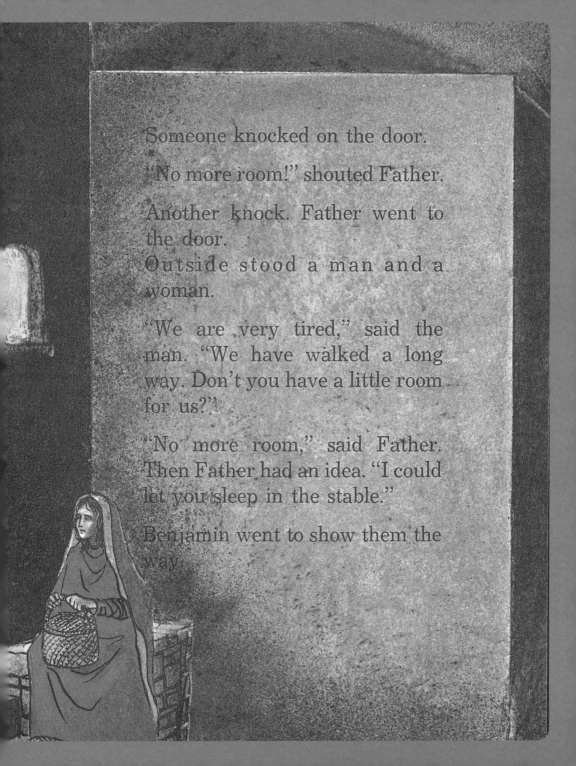

Someone knocked on the door.

"No more room!" shouted Father.

Another knock. Father went to the door.
Outside stood a man and a woman.

"We are very tired," said the man. "We have walked a long way. Don't you have a little room for us?"

"No more room," said Father. Then Father had an idea. "I could let you sleep in the stable."

Benjamin went to show them the way.

Through the courtyard he guided them, past sleepy travelers, to the stable.

The animals in the stable looked up as they came in and watched Benjamin pile fresh hay in a corner for the man and woman to sleep on.

"What's your name?" the man asked him.

"Benjamin," he answered.

"My name is Joseph," said the man, "and this is Mary, my wife. It took us five days to get here from Nazareth on foot."

Soon the town quieted down. The weary visitors and the tired townspeople all slept.

Benjamin was dreaming of all the crowds he had
seen that day.

Suddenly, something awakened him. He ran to the window. A very bright star was rising in the sky. Everything was quiet except for the cry of a baby. But there was a light in the stable. Benjamin rubbed his eyes. Were there people going into the stable?

In a flash Benjamin slipped out of the
room, out of the inn, out to the stable.
There he saw an amazing sight.

On the hay which Benjamin himself
had put in the manger for the animals, lay a beautiful, newborn baby.
Mary and Joseph were watching
over the baby. And close by knelt a
group of shepherds.

"What are those shepherds doing here?" Benjamin asked himself. "And why are they kneeling?"

One of the shepherds beckoned to him.
The shepherd was a rough looking fel-
low. Benjamin was just a bit afraid of
him.

But the man said, "Come in and see! It's the Prince of Peace!" The man's voice was so full of wonder that Benjamin forgot his fear.

"A Prince?" Benjamin asked. "But He's just a baby and in a stable."

"As we were watching our sheep tonight" the shepherd said, "suddenly an angel came to us. We were terribly frightened. But then the angel said:

'Be not afraid . . . I bring you good news . . . for to you is born this day in the city of David a Savior, who is Christ the Lord. And this will be a sign for you: you will find a Babe . . . lying in a manger.'

"Then came many more angels, all singing praise to God."

As soon as they went away, we went and found this stable. Here is the Baby in a manger just as the angel said!"

So this Baby was the Savior, the Prince
of Peace for whom Benjamin and his
father and his grandfather and his great-
grandfather had waited all these years.
Benjamin stepped forward to see the
little Christ Child better.

Then he knelt down. He thought of what his father had read that evening:

"The people who walked in darkness have seen a great light. . . . For to us a Child is born . . . the Prince of Peace."

Dear Parents:

The story tries to tell about the coming of the Christ Child the way a small Jewish boy of Jesus' time would have seen it. It tries to show how very much and why he would have been waiting for it. It reminds us how he would have been surprised to see the great Prince Messiah, the Lord Christ, as a baby in the place where he put food each day for the domestic animals.

By and large the people of Jesus' day expected the Messiah, or the Lord Christ, to come with kingly power and glory. His coming as their humble brother went against all they had expected. God's ways are so different from ours.

One of the promises God made about the Messiah was that His would be a kingdom with true peace between men, nature, and God (Is. 9:6, 7; 11:1-10). There was no agreement among the Jewish people how this would come about. The New Testament sees the peace which God offers in Jesus Christ as the coming of the Messiah's kingdom of peace and the brotherly love in Christ's church as part of it. When Jesus returns in glory, all evil will be destroyed. Then the dream of Benjamin and of his father and grandfather will come true.

Can you help your child to see the true meaning of Christmas, with its wonder over the love of God which made the Lord Christ want to share the humblest and commonest way of life, the love which brings peace from God and makes peace among men possible? You may want to read to your child (or help him read it himself) the story of Jesus' birth in your Bible. (Luke 2:1-20)

The Editor

QUALITY RELIGIOUS BOOKS FOR CHILDREN

ARCH BOOKS

Jon and the Little Lost Lamb

The Parable of the Good Shepherd

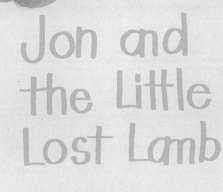

Jon and the Little Lost Lamb

LUKE 15:1-7 FOR CHILDREN

Written by Jane Latourette

Illustrated by Betty Wind

Concordia Publishing House

Inside the sheepfold, fast asleep,
What do you see? One hundred sheep!
That little one is "Baby Baa,"
who loves to snuggle in a heap
beside his brothers on the straw.

The morning sun is peeking in
to waken Baby Baa, who's been
a-dreaming of the meadow grass
that grows up where the hills begin,
right near the narrow mountain pass.

Since now another day's begun,
who comes along but Jonathan,
the shepherd, who unlocks the door,
and counts each sheep to see that none
is missing or is sick or sore?

One hundred strong, all safe and sound,
come greet the sun, as out they bound.
And little Baby Baa runs, too,
his tiny hoofs beat on the ground—
until he spies a plant to chew.

The shepherd lets them frisk and play,
before he leads them on their way
to meadows green, quite far from home —
good Jonathan knows every day
just where it's best to graze and roam.

At times it can be dangerous,
    as through the narrow mountain pas
    they walk along in single file —

(Now, Baa, don't be so *mischievous!*)
so Jon is watching all the while
to see that wolves aren't waiting there
about to spring down from their lair.

What's that? A lion sees the flock!
The shepherd, with no time to spare,
hurls with his sling a well-aimed rock.

He hits the beast between the eyes.
The lion falls. Stone-still he lies;
he's harmless now. Say, look ahead —
green, juicy grass! Their spirits rise,
and as they eat, Jon has his bread.

His kindly eyes keep in full view
his flock of sheep, who romp and chew,
or rest beneath the big tree's shade.
Let's see what Jon's about to do —
sweet music on the flute he made!

The hours go by, the sun sinks low;
it must be time for them to go
along the path for home again.
The shepherd calls, and in a row
he leads them downhill toward their pen.

They reach the fold, the shepherd counts
the sheep as through the door they bounce
to find a soft spot on the straw.
But wait! Just ninety-nine? He frowns—
oh, *where* is little Baby Baa?

How sad is our good shepherd Jon;
one lamb is lost or strayed. It's gone.
Jon's tired from tending sheep all day —
but he must search up hill and down
and find this lamb who's lost his way.

Jon climbs back to the pasture ground,
keeps calling, looking all around —
until beyond the place they'd stayed
he hears a little bleat that sounds
so low and faint and sore afraid.

You see, this lamb forgot and strayed
from his good shepherd late that day.
He did not hear Jon's call to come
and get in line for walking home,
so Baby Baa just romped and played.

But then he stumbled, tumbled down
into a hole — Would he be found?
The day turned slowly into night;
no shepherd near. What was that sound?
A jackal's howl — Baa froze with fright.

Another sound — his shepherd's voice!
Above the wild beast's night-time noise.
Baa's gently lifted up by Jon;
what happy reason to rejoice!
So safe at last, all fear is gone.

Once back inside the snug sheepfold,
the shepherd does not rant nor scold,
but smooths on olive oil to heal

all Baa's deep scratches, and we're told
it's done so kindly, Baa can feel
How much his shepherd cares for him —
one poor, lost lamb, back home again!

Dear Parents:

Our story is based on Jesus' parable of the Lost Sheep, a companion-story to His parables of the Lost Son and Lost Coin. All of these stories were told by Jesus to explain why He bothered about lost men. (Luke 15:1, 2)

"My attitude is like that of a good shepherd," Jesus says in this parable. God's feelings are just like the shepherd's: he is not satisfied with still having the "ninety-nine." The lostness of the one sheep does not let him rest. His joy over finding a stray sheep is even greater than any satisfaction over his having many sheep who are not lost.

Will you help your child see that Jesus is like the shepherd of our story? That He cares about and loves all God's children, even those who have been bad? That He does not leave them, nor does He want *us* to leave them, to their foolishness but rather brings them back home with joy? He is the "good shepherd Jonathan."

THE EDITOR

QUALITY RELIGIOUS BOOKS FOR CHILDREN

ARCH
BOOKS

The Story of
NOAH'S ARK

THE STORY OF
NOAH'S ARK

GENESIS 6:5–9:17 FOR CHILDREN

Written by Jane Latourette

Illustrated by Sally Mathews

Concordia Publishing House

The Bible tells that long ago
God looked on earth and here below
saw all His creatures full of hate;
He asked, "Oh, *what* did I create?

"Why *do* my people war and fight,
when they've been told
about what's right?
They don't seem sorry for their ways
nor *want* to change to better days."

God thought awhile and then declared:
"The only one that can be spared
is Noah, who, it's plain to see,
has lived in peace, with his sons three.

"But every other living thing
will be destroyed by covering
the whole, wide world
with floods so great
I'll sweep away
the fear and hate."

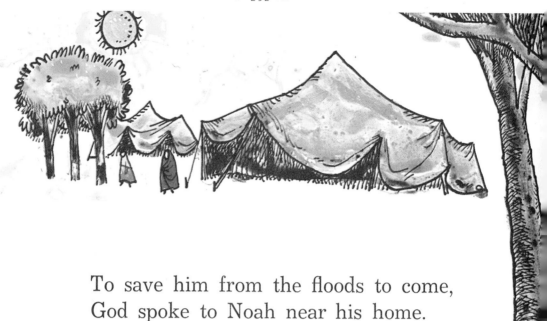

To save him from the floods to come,
God spoke to Noah near his home.
An ark he must start building now,
four hundred feet from stern to prow,
three stories high, and extra wide,
with door, and windows on each side.

"It must be big, since in this boat
you'll need to keep yourself afloat —
your wife and sons and wives; then bring
a pair of every living thing
that creeps or crawls or runs or flies.
What space you'll need just for supplies!"

Shem, Japheth, Ham, the grown sons, three,
found each was willing to agree

and started building this great ark,
all working hard from dawn till dark.

They heard their neighbors
laugh and jeer
and say, "What crazy folks, and queer —
to build a boat on high, dry land!"
They just refused to understand.

The ark took many years to build.
God watched and waited
till they filled

the ship with all the needed things
for months of water voyaging.

Much food and clothing,
pots and plants
were stowed aboard.
They took no chance
of starving either beasts or men
while on the ark for weeks on end.

Next, Noah's search was not in vain:
from mountain, jungle, hill, and plain
he led the creatures two by two,
the tigers, bears, and kangaroo,
the horses, goats, and porcupines,
all trailing in in two long lines.

The sky was dark
with flapping wings;
the ground was 'live
with creeping things;

earth trembled at the mighty roar
of beasts all moving
toward the door.

Then Noah's wife and sons and wives
went up the ramp. They dried their eyes.
And as the sun shone hot about,
they heard the people laugh and shout.

Aboard at last! The rains did come;

they beat the roof with steady drum
for forty days and forty nights
as bit by bit land sank from sight.

The tops of mountains disappeared
as Noah from his windows peered.
An awesome sight, to look around
and see no trace of your home ground!

Can you imagine how you'd feel
to hear the thunder's crashing peal,
and pitch
    and toss
        in wind and storm —
the *only* ones alive and warm?

For six long months
on board they stayed.
It was not easy, but they prayed
that God would see them safely through
until dry land
came back in view.

The rains did stop; the flood went down
until the ark bumped on the crown
of mountain tall called Ararat,
and there the ship stuck fast, just sat.

Soon Noah let a raven go,
a big, black bird, which to and fro
went flying, finding food afloat
as they all watched it from the boat.

God sent strong winds the earth to dry,
yet still the waters seemed so high!
A dove flew next to look around
but did not find unflooded ground.

A week went by, and out again
this time the dove — oh, joy, amen! —
brought back a fresh-plucked olive leaf,
a sign of life! Oh, what relief!

Another week, the dove once more
was sent abroad to search, explore.
This time she did not reappear,
which meant that dry land
must be near.

The earth was drying rapidly,
and soon they found that they were free
to leave the ark. This happy throng
burst into sounds of joy and song.

To show their thanks
that they were spared,
the people built an altar there.
And God was pleased as He looked on;
He blessed good Noah and his sons.

To them He said, "Go build new homes;
have children who in turn will roam
and settle countries far and near.
Another flood you need not fear.

"To show you that My promise will
be kept forever, see that hill?
Beyond it I have placed up high
a lovely rainbow in the sky.

"By this fair sign will people know
My promise will be kept. So go
with faith to plant the earth again."
To this old Noah said,
"Amen!"

Dear Parents:

The world God made enjoyed peace with God, and there was harmony between creatures. But soon things became different. The Bible tells us that when God saw the violence on the earth, He decided to blot out both man and beast; He was sorry that He had made them. (Gen. 6:6, 7, 11-13)

But God decided to save Noah, a blameless man who walked with God, and through him give another chance to His creatures. So the story of God's judging the earth becomes the story of His saving it.

Christians have always seen Noah's ark as a picture of the salvation in Christ offered to us in Baptism (1 Peter 3:20, 21) and in the life of the Christian church, pictured as a ship on the stormy seas.

Will you help your child see the real meaning of the story? This is a story of God's caring and of His saving His creatures from the destruction that disobedience brings.

Whenever your child sees it raining, he should remember the promise God gave with the rainbow.

THE EDITOR

QUALITY RELIGIOUS BOOKS FOR CHILDREN

ARCH BOOKS

THE WORLD GOD MADE

THE STORY OF CREATION

Written by Alyce Bergey
Illustrated by Obata Studio

THE WORLD GOD MADE

THE STORY OF CREATION

GENESIS 1 and 2 FOR CHILDREN

Concordia Publishing House

Once there was no world.

There were no people.

There were no animals.

There were no hills and no trees.

There was no sky and no sun.

There was no world at all!

It

was

very,

very

dark.

God said, "I'll make a world!"
And so God made the world.
He made the world long, long ago.

God said, "Let there be light!"
And there was light.
God called the light Day.
He called the dark time Night.
God saw the light that He had made.
He said, "This is good!"

Then God said, "I'll make the skies!"
God made the sky.
He made the sky blue
and put white clouds in it to hold the rain.
God said, "I'll make the seas and lakes,
the rivers and dry land."
God made the seas and lakes and rivers.

After that He made the dry land.
God called the land Earth.
He put the land in some places.
He put the seas
and lakes and rivers in other places.
God saw the water and the land.
He said, "This is good!"

Then God began to make things
to grow on the earth.
God said, "Let there be grass!"
And there was grass.
God said, "Let there be trees!"
And there were trees.
The grass and the trees
made the earth
green and bright.
God said, "Let there be
plants and flowers!"
And there were
plants and flowers.
God made red flowers
and white flowers
and yellow flowers.
God made plants and flowers
of every shape and color.
God saw that the flowers
made the earth very pretty.
And the plants grew good things
to eat.
God said, "This is good!"

God said, "Let there be lights
to shine in the sky."
God made the sun.
God made the moon.
He made the stars, too.

God put them in the sky:
the sun to shine in the day,
the moon and the stars
to shine at night.
God saw the sun, the moon,
and the stars.
God said, "This is good!"

Then God said,

"Let there be birds

to fly in the sky."

"Let there be fish to swim in th

seas, the lakes and rivers.

God made whales
and every animal
that lives in the water.

Then God said,
"Let there be animals on the earth."

He made animals that hop
and animals that jump.
God made animals that walk
and animals that crawl.

"Have many little ones,"
He said to all the animals.

Now the world
was ready for people.
God said, "I'll make a man.
I'll make him like Myself.
I'll have him rule over the earth."
So God made the first man.
God made him from clay
He took from the earth,
breathed on him,
and called him Adam.
God made man
a little like Himself.
God said to him,
"You shall rule over the earth
and everything that walks
or crawls, swims or flies!"
Then God planted a garden.
It was a very pretty garden.
God planted grass and trees
and flowers in it.
He gave the garden to Adam.
It was Adam's home,
and he was to look after it.
God took all the animals to Adam.
God said, "Give each one a name."
So Adam began
to name the animals.

God had made a little animal
that had a house on its back.
Adam named it Turtle.

God had made a very tall animal
with a long, long neck.
Adam named it Giraffe.

God had made an animal with long ears
and a little round tail.
Adam named it Rabbit.

God had made a very big animal
that looked like it had two tails.
Adam named it Elephant.

And Adam named the frog and the fox,
the horse and the bear.
He named every animal that God had made.

All the animals came in twos,
but Adam was all alone.
There were no other people!

God said, "It is not good
for man to be alone."
So God made a lady.
He brought her to Adam.
Adam named the lady Eve.

God made Adam and Eve to live together.
(That's why people get married
and have families.)

God blessed Adam and Eve and said,
"Have children and grandchildren!
Let people fill the earth and rule it!"

In six days God had made the world.
On the seventh day He rested
from all His work.

God saw all the things He had made.
And God said, "This is very good!"

Dear Parents:

The story of the creation in the Bible is about the world as God made it and intended it to be. God's world was full of wonders, infinite variety, color, and harmony. God made it with much care and love and joy. The Creator presented it to man to rule it, take care of it, and enjoy it (the story of the garden of Eden). Man was the crowning piece of God's creation. He resembled God Himself, for he was made in the image of God. He was to live in community with the world's Creator, with his own human counterpart (counterparts), and with nature. He was blessed with work and with carefree rest, as God Himself is portrayed to have first worked and then rested. He was given the gift of being able to have a family.

Can you help your child appreciate the wonderful work and plan of God which he meets every day? Can you help him see how God continues, preserves, and saves His creation from the evil powers which try to destroy His work?

You could read Psalm 8 with your child and possibly learn it by heart with him. You could also have him make a scrapbook or a paper wall hanging illustrating parts of the great Creation Psalm, Psalm 104.

THE EDITOR

ARCH BOOKS

THE Little BOAT
That Almost Sank

How Jesus Stopped The Storm

THE Little BOAT That Almost Sank

Matthew 14:22-33
Mark 6:45-51

FOR CHILDREN

Written by Mary Warren
Illustrated by Kveta Rada

Concordia Publishing House

"I am tired," said Jesus
to His friends one evening.

"I will send the crowds away,
and then I must go into the hills alone
to talk to God.
You men row across the lake in your boat,
and I will meet you after a while."

The sun had set
like an enormous red balloon

floating down to the edge of the sky.

And now the birds tucked their heads
under their wings to sleep;

and the flowers folded themselves
quietly for the night;
and the stars prickled their sparkly way
into the great, black blanket of night.

Peter raised his hands in prayer.

"I will shove the boat off,"
said James to his friends
as they took up the oars.

The only sound was the soft sound
of wind whooshing the waves
and the soft slap of oars dipping in water.

"The wind is getting worse," said John
after they had rowed for a bit.
"We want to make our boat go one way,
but the wind is starting
to push it the other way."

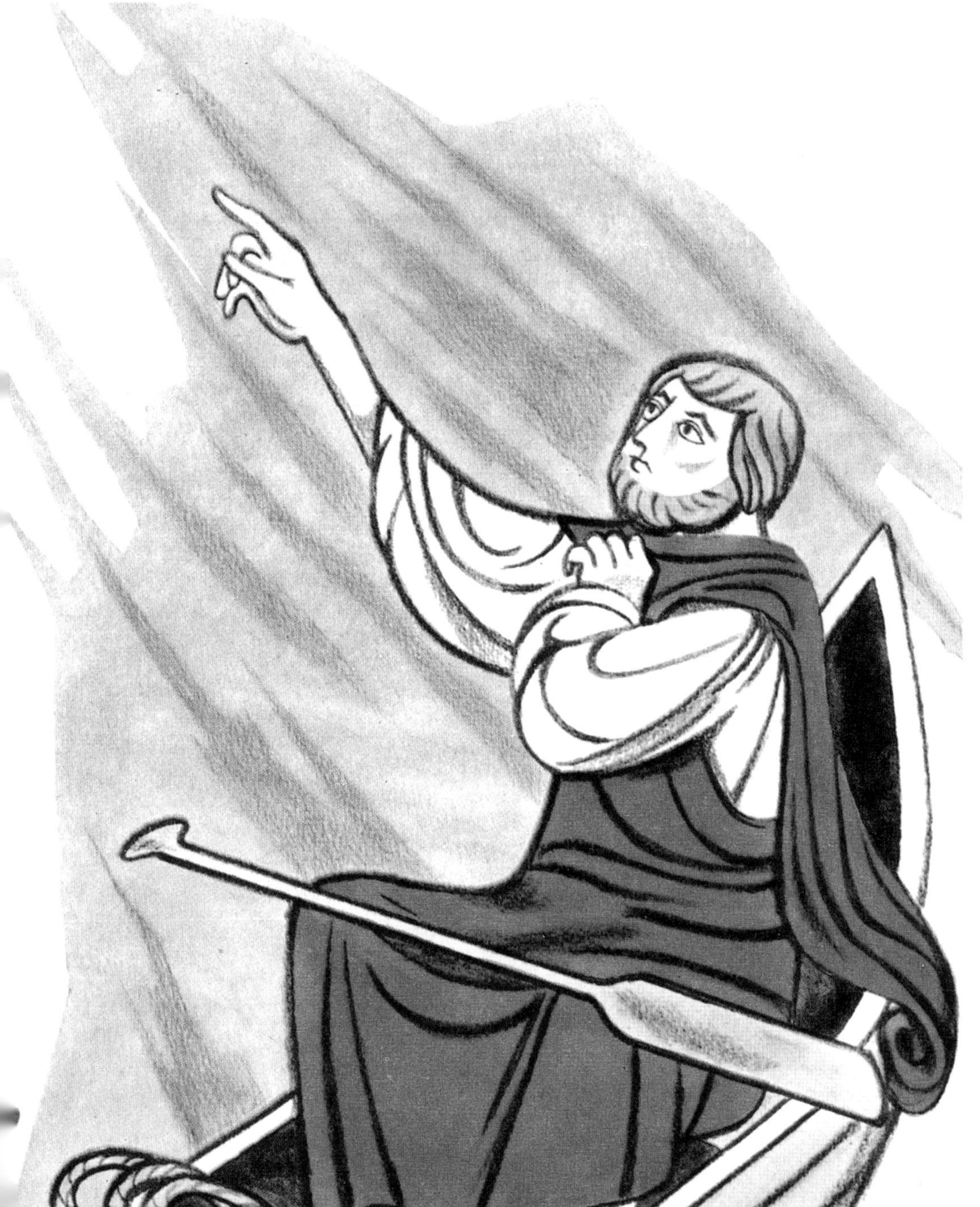

By then the sound of the wind had become
like the roar of an angry lion.
The little waves turned to big waves,
and the big waves
thumped and bumped and rocked the boat
and splashed water into it.

"I'm scared!" shouted Andrew
above the noise of the wind
and the boom of the waves.

"I am a fisherman
and have been in rough water many times.
But this is terrible! I'm scared!"

"I am, too!" shouted Peter.
"If Jesus were here, I would not feel so scared."

"I wish He had come with us!"
called another man, wet and trembling
and afraid.

When Jesus looked out from the top of the hill,
He could see the boat rocking in the moonlight
and all of the men pulling hard at the oars.

"That is a strong wind!" He said to Himself.
"It is the middle of the night,
and they are getting nowhere.
They must be wet and cold and frightened."

Down the hill went Jesus,
down the hill and over the rocks,
down in the dark

until He got to the shore.

The wind hissed and the waves roared
and the boat rocked and the men trembled —
afraid!

Then they saw Jesus —
walking toward them on the water!
They were stiff with fear.
"A ghost!" they screamed.
"The storm is bad enough.
But now — a ghost!"

But over the hiss of the wind
and the boom of the waves
and the cries of the men
came a voice they knew:
"It is I! Do not be afraid!"

"O Jesus! Jesus!" called Peter,
"If that is really You, please tell me
to come to You on the water!"

In the darkness, above the roar of the wind, Jesus said quietly: "Come, Peter! Come!"

Peter climbed over the side of the boat
and, looking ahead at Jesus, he felt brave.
He took some steps out on the water,
but suddenly the waves thundered in his ears,
and instead of looking at Jesus, he looked down.

"I cannot do it!" he thought to himself,
and he began to sink.
"Lord! Help!" he cried.
Jesus quickly stretched His arm and caught him.
"Peter! Peter!
You thought you could not do it?
Why don't you have more faith in Me?"

Together they climbed into the boat.
The wind stopped roaring
and the waves stopped pounding
and the boat stopped rocking,
and there came again
the gentle whoosh of the waves
and the soft slap of the oars
dipping in water.

"Jesus!"
whispered Peter and Andrew and all of the men.
"You can make a storm go away!
You can make the winds hush!
When You are with us,
we are not afraid."

Dear Parents:

This story is a story of awe and wonder over the mysterious and kingly power of the Lord Christ: "Who is He whom even the waves and winds obey?"

To the people of the Bible, much more exposed to the mercy of the elements than our city man of today, the "waters" and the wind were not just uncontrollable; they were also mysterious and often frightening. When describing the greatness of God's power, they loved to picture Him as mastering the water and the wind — driving them, blowing, walking, sitting, riding upon them — or rescuing His people from them (e.g., Exodus 14:21, 22; 15:8-11; Psalm 18:6-19; 29; 77:14-19). He who is more powerful than the elements is the Master of the universe and the Savior of His people. He is stronger than all the forces that would do us harm. There is no need to lose heart when He is near.

Peter sensed this and ventured out toward his Lord outside the boat. But then he made a mistake we all do. Instead of looking at his Lord he was distracted by the strong wind. He lost his nerve and the "ground" under his feet. But Jesus did not let him sink.

Will you help your child think of Jesus as this story pictures Him?

THE EDITOR

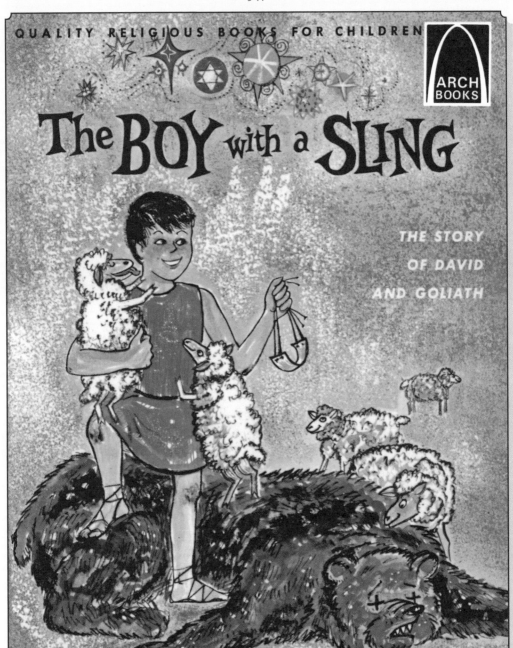

QUALITY RELIGIOUS BOOKS FOR CHILDREN

ARCH BOOKS

The BOY with a SLING

THE STORY
OF DAVID
AND GOLIATH

The Boy
with
a SLING

1 SAMUEL 16:1—18:5 FOR CHILDREN

Written by
Mary Warren

Illustrated by
Sally Mathews

Concordia Publishing House

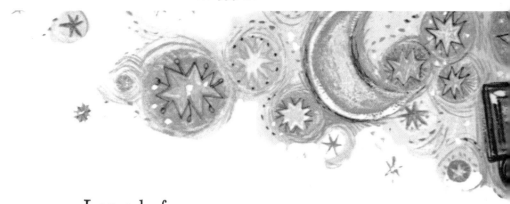

Long before
Mary or Joseph or Jesus were born,
God said to Samuel, His priest,
"Put oil in your horn,
and go now and find
the Bethlehem boy I have in mind
to be king of my people some day."

It was to the home of Jesse
that Samuel went.
After meeting and greeting his sons,
he asked:
"Are there more?"
And so Jesse sent
to the fields for his youngest,
David the shepherd boy,
handsome and strong.

God said to Samuel:
"You are looking for one to be king —
this is he!
Take holy oil, anoint him for Me!"

Nobody knew
except God and His holy man, Samuel,
what this would do.
Alone on the hills, he had to keep
lions and bears from stealing his sheep,
and the Spirit of God gave him such
courage and might
that the wildest of creatures
he dared to fight!

There was at this time a long war.
The Philistine army
and the Israelites, under King Saul,
camped on two mountains.

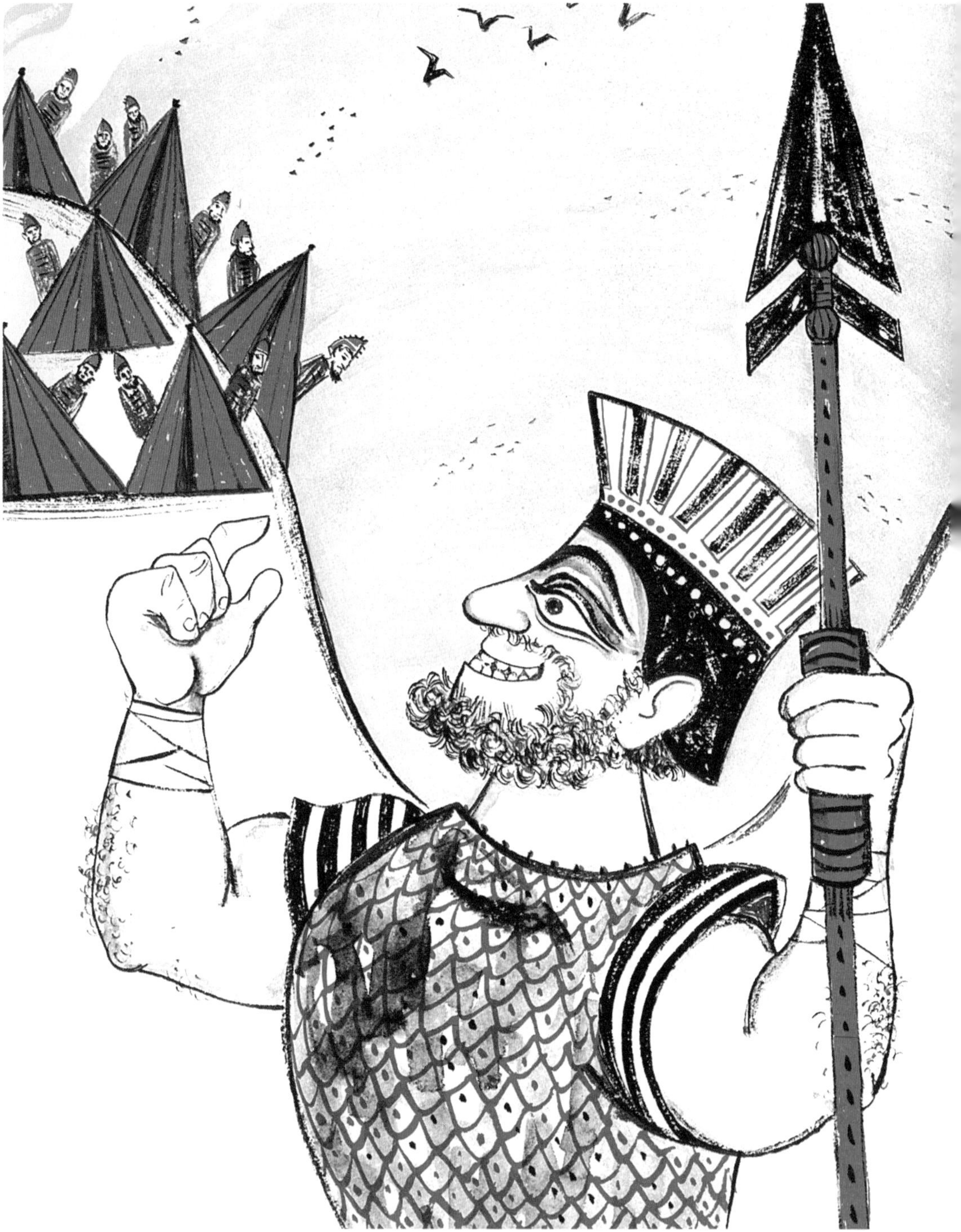

Each morning a Philistine giant,
Goliath of Gath,
came down in the Valley of Elah to call
"Is any man there
who will fight against me?
I shall chop off his head
and cut up his body like bread
to toss to the beasts
and the birds!
WHO WILL DARE?"

Goliath the giant put fear
in each Israelite heart with his shout.
His brass armor clinked; his long spear
made even the bravest men doubt
that any could fight him and win.

One day the shepherd boy, David, came
with cheese and some bread
for his brothers
who fought in Saul's army.
Like the others, they ran
when Goliath came down.

When David saw this,
he said with a frown:
"Goliath makes fun of our God!
Does no one believe that the Lord
takes care of His armies in need?

"I will fight this giant
myself!"

King Saul heard of David's brave words.
He sent for the boy and he smiled.
"You are hardly more than a child!
Goliath knows all about war!
What are *you* offering for?"

Said David: "Out in the field
when either a lion or bear
tried to steal my father's young sheep,
my God helped me fight with him there.
I know in this battle God will
shield and deliver me still!"

Saul put his armor on David:
"Here is my coat of mail . . .
my helmet . . . my very own sword.
Go! In the name of the Lord!"

But Saul's armor was heavy; he fell.
"I cannot wear them, O King!
I am used to only a sling!"

With his sling and his shepherd's crook
David stopped to search at the brook
for some stones.
With these in his bag, he went on
to the place where Goliath of Gath
made the Israelites tremble in fear.
"Who is there?" roared Goliath.

His shield bearer stood before him, but he
was still able to see
David the shepherd boy. And with a sneer
and a laugh that was cruel,
Goliath drew near.

"Why do you pick
such a boy for this fight?
Am I but a dog to be chased with a stick?
Come! I will throw all your bones
to the birds of the air
and the beasts of the field!"

David reached for his stones.
"Your spear is sharp and long and strong;
your shield is great and heavy too.
There is one reason that I came.
You mock the Lord and . . . in His name
I have power to conquer you!"

David's hand dipped in his bag.
Before Goliath had time to see
he put a stone in his sling and — WHEE!

It hit the Philistine in the head;

he staggered, then fell forward —

Goliath was DEAD.

David ran with a glorious shout
and took the giant's heavy sword
and cut his head off. Soon the word
spread through the Philistine camp.
The men raced hard to get away
but the Israelites were close behind
and many Philistines died that day.

Triumphantly they marched to bring
the battle news and Goliath's head
to Saul, the waiting king, who said:
"Your strength from God, O David, wins
Israel this victory;
my army needs such bravery!"

From that day on young David stayed
at court with Saul, who knew he'd need
a captain who was strong to lead
his men in other battles too.

This army training helped him grow
to be, in time, God's chosen king —
he who once had been a boy
who killed a giant with a sling!

Dear Parents:

The story of David and Goliath is so loved by all children because here a "big bully," the giant Goliath, gets outsmarted and defeated by the "little guy," David.

In a way this story stands for the entire history of the People of God. God surprises us again and again by the instruments He chooses: the little nation Israel, the timid Moses (Exodus 4:10-16), the young shepherd boy David, the little nobody Mary, the simple fishermen, the unimpressive speaker Paul (1 Corinthians 2:1-5). God gives His Spirit and power to the least likely people and changes the lives of men and of nations through them.

It is really not David or Moses or any of the important figures of the Bible who is the "hero," but God, who saves His People through them, who "resists the proud" and is the Champion of the oppressed. It is He who gives power to the powerless, wisdom to the simple, and opens up new possibilities where men see only a dead end.

Will you help your child understand this as you talk over the story, and lead him to believe it by the way you yourself deal with the pressures and anxieties of life?

THE EDITOR

QUALITY RELIGIOUS BOOKS FOR CHILDREN

ARCH
BOOKS

THE BABY BORN IN A STABLE

THE BABY BORN IN A STABLE

LUKE 2:1-18 FOR CHILDREN

Written by Janice Kramer

Illustrated by Dorse Lampher

Concordia Publishing House

Not quite two thousand years ago
the emperor decreed
that all the world must be enrolled....
LET NO ONE FAIL TO HEED.

(The world was quite mixed up, you see,
and no one seemed to know:
how many people WERE there? And
what taxes did they owe?)

Throughout the earth the rich,
the poor, the young, the very old,
all traveled to their towns of birth
so they could be enrolled.

And so it was, to Bethlehem
a man named Joseph went
to list his name and see how much
he owed the government.
Beside him Mary traveled, too.
Not once did she protest
how long and hard the trip had been,
how much she needed rest.

In Bethlehem they found the inn
and knocked upon the door.
"My rooms are filled!" the owner yelled,
"I haven't any more!"
When Joseph told him quietly
of gentle Mary's plight:
that she would have a baby soon,
perhaps that very night,

the owner stood in thought and rubbed
his bushy bearded jaw.
"I'll let you have the stable, then.
You'll have to sleep on straw."

So Joseph and his wife unpacked
and settled down to rest
not caring that they couldn't have
the biggest and the best.
They ate their supper slowly as
they watched the sun go down,
and yawned as darkness fell at last
upon the little town.

The night was silent. Everyone,
it seemed, was fast asleep
except for shepherds in the fields
who had to watch their sheep.
They huddled close and whispered low
to keep themselves awake.

Then suddenly their eyes grew wide —
their knees began to shake.
For there, above them in the sky,
an angel did appear.
The glory of the Lord shone down,
and they were filled with fear.

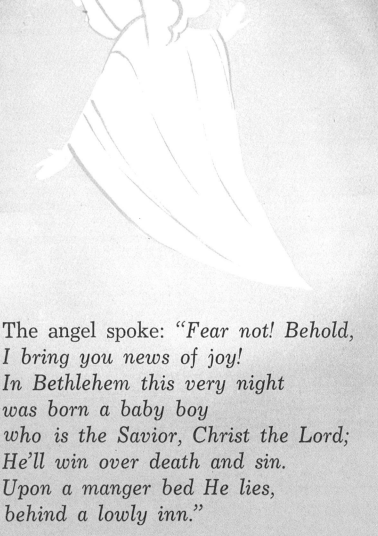

The angel spoke: "*Fear not! Behold,
I bring you news of joy!
In Bethlehem this very night
was born a baby boy
who is the Savior, Christ the Lord;
He'll win over death and sin.
Upon a manger bed He lies,
behind a lowly inn.*"

And suddenly a multitude
of angels filled the sky,
their voices glorifying God
and praising Him on high!
And "*Peace on earth, good will to men!*"
resounded through the air —
it seemed there must have been at least
a million angels there!

No longer did the shepherds quake
with anxious fear and dread,
and when the angels disappeared
the shepherds quickly said:
"Oh, let us go to Bethlehem
and find the manger bed!"
And off across the fields they ran —
to Bethlehem they sped!

The manger wasn't hard to find,
and there the shepherds' eyes
fell on a sight that filled their hearts
with wonder and surprise:

For there was Joseph, standing tall
and gazing down with care
upon his blessed Mary and
the baby lying there.

"A wondrous child!" the shepherds cried
in voices of delight.
"See there — around him shines a strange
and heav'nly looking light.
How warm and bright it seems against
the coldness of this night!
He surely is the one we seek;
the angel's words were right!"

To Mary and to Joseph and
to everyone they saw
the shepherds told the story that
had filled them with such awe:
"This baby is the Promised Prince,
        the Mighty Lord,
        the King.

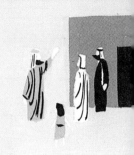

We know because tonight we heard
the holy angels sing.
They told us that this blessed child
of low and humble birth
was truly Christ, the Son of God,
the Savior of the earth!"

The news was spread from town
to town.

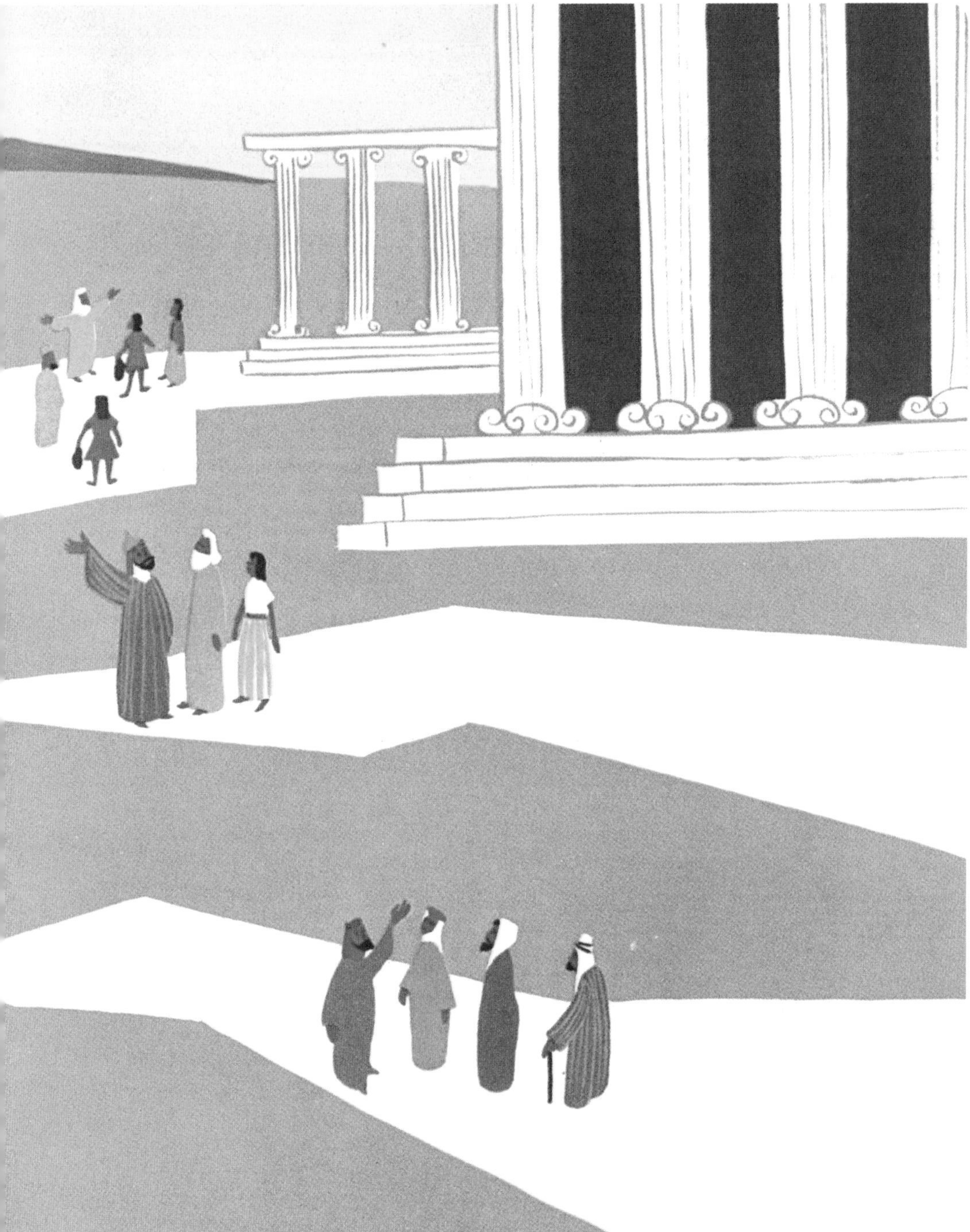

The whole world must be told
till every person,

rich

or young

or poor

or very old,

has heard about the coming of
the Savior of all men,
whom God has sent to earth because
of His great love for them.

A CHILD'S CHRISTMAS PRAYER

Be near me, Lord Jesus;

I ask Thee to stay

close by me forever,

and love me, I pray.

Bless all the dear children

in Thy tender care,

and take us to heaven

to live with Thee there.

DEAR PARENTS:

Have you ever had the feeling that your child is confused at Christmastime? There is such a mixture of reindeer, Santa Claus, presents, parties, angels, and unreal mangers. What are we really celebrating, and why? How did it all happen?

Our book is intended to help parents and children remember the real story of the first Christmas and the love of God behind it. Our heavenly Father sent us a Savior who did not shrink from being poor and unrecognized. Christ wasn't even born in a house. We often forget this and tend to be too romantic about the manger in the stable. Mary and Joseph had a hard time of it! The shepherds who welcomed the Christ Child were the nobodies of society in that day. Our God chooses hard and strange ways to win back His children. This is why Jesus came. He saves us from the power of sin and brings God's life back to us.

This is the Good News, and really the only reason we celebrate Christmas. Without it we would have only empty trimmings. Will you help your child see the heart of Christmas by making the first Christmas come alive for him and by centering the season in the birth of Christ?

THE EDITOR